Amazing
AIRPLANES

Introduction by
Chuck Yeager

Written by Regen Dennis

*Illustrations by Sylvia Shapiro
and Andi Rusu*

Andrews and McMeel
A Universal Press Syndicate Company
Kansas City

To Bruce, my personal airplane expert, who kept my wings aloft. Thanks to Claire Dederer, my editor, who made this project great fun.
—R. D.

Amazing Airplanes copyright © 1995 by becker&mayer!, Ltd. All rights reserved. Printed in Canada. No part of this book may be used or reproduced in any manner whatsoever without written permission except in the case of reprints in the context of reviews. For information, write Andrews and McMeel, a Universal Press Syndicate Company, 4900 Main Street, Kansas City, Missouri 64112.

From the *Amazing Airplanes Book & Kit* packaged set, which includes balsa wood airplanes and this book.

ISBN: 0-8362-4241-6

The *Amazing Airplanes Book & Kit* packaged set is produced by becker&mayer!, Ltd.
Cover, package, and interior color illustrations: Sylvia Oltion Shapiro
Interior line illustrations: Andi Rusu
Design and composition: Suzanne Brooker
Advisors: Greg Moyce and Brian Baum of the Museum of Flight, Seattle WA

Special thanks to Jim Porter for his help in designing the airplanes.

Other children's kits from Andrews and McMeel by becker&mayer!

The Amazing Sandcastle Builder's Kit	The English Thoroughbred
The Ant Book & See-Through Model	Fun with Ballet
Build Your Own Dinosaurs	Fun with Electronics
Build Your Own Bugs	Sleeping Beauty
The American Appaloosa	

INTRODUCTION

It was really exciting to be the first person ever to fly faster than the speed of sound. Before that flight, I spent a lot of time in the air, experimenting with different controls and flying techniques. When everything finally came together, breaking the sound barrier was a real thrill. Experimenting is what flying is all about. Once you understand the basics of flight and you've assembled your airplanes, try different ways to make them fly higher and longer. Don't be afraid to try something new—move the wings up or back, try a different toss, or even create your own one-of-a-kind airplane. Watch your airplanes in flight to figure out what you can do to make them fly better. Who knows, you might even hear a sonic boom! Keep on experimenting, just like I did.

General Chuck Yeager
United States Air Force, Ret.

How to Assemble Your Planes

You should have:
a bag of colored clips
2 propellers
2 landing gears
4 rubber bands
clay
4 wire hooks
6 sheets of balsa wood
2 balsa wood fuselages

Look carefully at the colored plastic clips. They have narrow slots and wide slots. You'll be using the narrow slots in subassembly to join individual parts. The wide slots will attach your subassembly parts to the airplane fuselage in final assembly.

Now that you've opened the box and spilled airplane parts all over the floor, you're ready to get started! But before you start building airplanes, let's take a look at the parts of an airplane and what they're called:

These directions show you how to build eight airplanes the same way Boeing, McDonnell Douglas, and Airbus build airplanes: first subassembly, then final assembly. Subassembly means putting together individual pieces to create big sections such as the tail or the wings, so that when you're ready for final assembly, all you have to do is pop the sections onto the fuselage and fly away.

Make sure you have everything. You should have five sheets of balsa wood airplane parts and two thick fuselages. Part of the challenge of subassembly is finding the right parts.

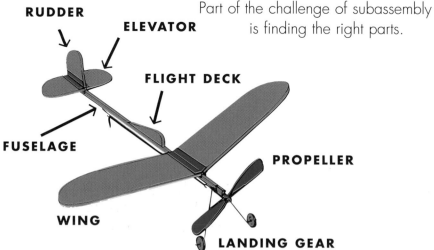

RUDDER
ELEVATOR
FLIGHT DECK
FUSELAGE
PROPELLER
WING
LANDING GEAR

YES   NO

SUBASSEMBLY OF THE WINGS

The plane will fly best if you snap the wings with the long edges facing in the same direction.

Snap matching wings into the narrow slots of the clips like this:

Two wings #3 into the red clip.

Two wings #1 into the dark blue clip.

Wings #4 & #7 into the dark green clip.

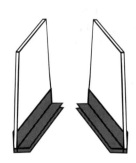

Wings #22 & #23 into the yellow clip.

Snap the fuselage extension #26 into the bottom of the dark blue clip. This looks pretty weird, but will make sense later.

Snap each winglet, #12 & #13, into a gray clip.

SUBASSEMBLY OF THE TAILS

This gets tricky because every tail is different. Start by pushing the small triangular wedges into the orange, purple, white, and black clips as shown. When you're attaching the rudders and elevators to the tail clip, make sure the wide part of the wedge faces toward the back of the clip.

Snap elevators #10 & #11 into opposite slots of the orange clip, and rudder #17 into the middle narrow slot.

Snap the elevators #8 & #9 and rudder #16 into the purple clip the same way.

Snap elevators #5 & #6 and rudder #20 into the white clip.

Snap elevators #14 & #15 and rudder #24 into the black clip, then attach the light green clips to the outside edges of the elevators and snap in two rudders #2.

This one's going to seem backward: Snap the wide part of rudder #21 into the pink clip and the narrow part of the same rudder into the brown clip. Now snap elevators #18 & #19 into the brown clip. It gets easier from here on.

AMAZING AIRPLANES

FUSELAGE

Fit the center of the landing gear into the groove on the propeller assembly.

Gently push the straight end of the wire hook into the underside of the fuselage, about 2" from the end of the tail, with the opening facing toward the back.

Take a rubber band and thread it through the wire loop on the back of the propeller, then tie a knot to make a loop. Pull the rubber band over the hook.

← 2" →

OTHER STUFF

You should have only a couple of parts left over: two light blue clips that look different from any of the other clips, two extra hooks, two extra rubber bands (in case you lose them!), and two small balsa wood parts—flight decks #25 and #27. Save them for final assembly.

Now you're ready for final assembly. The only other thing you'll need is clear tape. There are two fuselage sections, so you can build two airplanes at once. Final assembly directions are next to the story about each airplane. You're ready to fly!

SPIRIT OF ST. LOUIS

In his day Charles A. Lindbergh was probably considered a wild and crazy guy. He learned how to fly at an early age and did parachuting for fun, then became an airmail pilot, which was considered really daring and romantic in the 1920s.

By 1925, airplanes from around the world were criss-crossing the oceans and continents. But no one had been brave enough—or crazy enough, as Charles's parents probably thought—to fly across an ocean all alone, or SOLO. Then Lindbergh accepted a challenge: Fly solo across the Atlantic Ocean and earn a $25,000 prize and lots of honor and fame. Of course, there were big risks involved. If he didn't succeed, he'd have a long swim.

Lindbergh's airplane, the *Spirit of St. Louis*, was not much more complex than a 10-speed bike. It took only two months to build and measured just 28 feet long, much shorter than a bus. The *Spirit of St. Louis* was a MONOPLANE (one wing) with a fancy gas engine and hardly any instruments except for a COMPASS to show what direction it was headed and an ALTIMETER to show how high up it was.

Conspicuously missing were a radio and a windshield. Lindbergh needed so much fuel to make the long ocean crossing that he installed extra fuel tanks in front of and behind the pilot's seat. To see where he was going, he rigged up a periscope. The *Spirit of St. Louis* was really just a flying gas tank.

Being basically smart, Lindbergh waited for good weather, packed two canteens of water and five sandwiches, and took off not far from New York City. Thirty-three and a half hours later, he landed near Paris, very excited to get his hands on the prize money, get some sleep, and be interviewed by history-book writers who gave him the cool nickname, "The Lone Eagle."

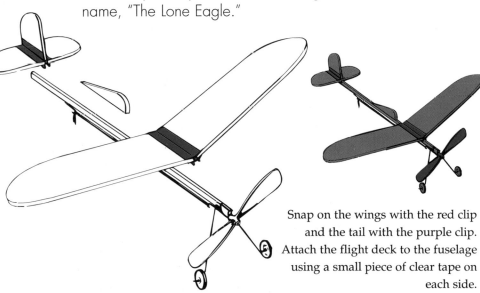

Snap on the wings with the red clip and the tail with the purple clip. Attach the flight deck to the fuselage using a small piece of clear tape on each side.

SOPWITH CAMEL

$\mathcal{A}$ biplane
with the weird name of
Sopwith Camel was the
superstar of air combat during World War I. Designed in
1917 by Sir Thomas Sopwith of Great Britain, it carried four
bombs and had two machine guns with humpback covers,
that might give you a clue how it got named. While the airplane's firepower made it vicious, what made the Camel
famous was its speed and agility—it could dance circles
around most other aircraft. The Sopwith Camel was introduced midway through the war and it quickly turned the
tide of victory to the Allied Forces. By winning more combat
victories—1,294 to be exact—and killing more enemy than

any other type of plane, the Sopwith Camel gave the Allies control of the air.

The Sopwith Camel's most famous rival was the German Fokker triplane, especially the gaudy red one flown by the Red Baron, who single-handedly downed more Allied airplanes, a lot of them Sopwith Camels, than anyone else.

Sopwith Camel pilots became the big-time heroes of World War I. Zipping along at about 113 miles per hour, all alone in the open cockpit, they startled enemy aircraft by darting above, below, and alongside them with amazing speed and maneuverability.

The Sopwith Camel may have an exciting combat record, but its safety record wasn't as dazzling. Pilots were in constant danger of the plane exploding if enemy fire hit their fuel tanks. Even worse, the engines had a tendency to stop, a nasty flaw in design that killed many student pilots during takeoff. But in wartime, danger just added excitement, so there was always a waiting list to fly the Sopwith Camel.

Connect the wings with the red clip, then the fuselage extension (with the dark blue clip) goes above the wings with the red clip. Tape the front and back ends of the fuselage extension to the fuselage. Snap on the tail with the purple clip.

CONSTELLATION

FUNKY FINS

The Constellation's engines were so powerful and large—propellers were 15 feet in diameter—that three large tail fins were needed to balance the airplane and keep it flying smoothly. The fins looked funky, too, and probably inspired automakers to put them on 1950s cars.

By the late 1930s, more and more people figured out that flying was quicker and easier than taking a train or driving a car. Especially when crossing oceans. To carry all these eager travelers, Lockheed began designing a big four-engine airplane with a flashy tail that could fly from continent to continent.

The Constellation is one of the first really modern airliners. It introduced nifty new features such as DE-ICING, to melt the ice that forms on the wings and tail. Another first was HYDRAULIC controls that move the flaps, ailerons, and elevators using pistons powered by the pressure from fluids, similar to the pressure you get by pushing water out of a squirt gun.

Before the Constellation ever took off as a passenger plane, World War II came along. Military leaders, thinking that airplanes were the best invention since gunpowder, needed large aircraft to move armies from place to place. It made sense to turn the Constellation into a military TRANSPORT.

After the war ended, most of the Constellations—nicknamed "Connies"—were sold to airlines, spruced up, and put into service on long flights. They were the first-class way to travel in those days.

A new, improved Super Constellation came along, followed a few years later by another model named the Starliner, considered the ultimate in airplanes. Unfortunately, just about then, jet airplanes were invented and all the airlines wanted faster, high-tech jetliners. But they couldn't find recycling bins big enough for their old Connies. Instead, they sold most of them to airlines in Central and South America where they were perfect for carrying passengers safely over vast jungles and mountains. Other old Constellations were bought by the military and made into spy planes named Warning Stars.

Snap on the wings with the red clip and the tail with the black clip.

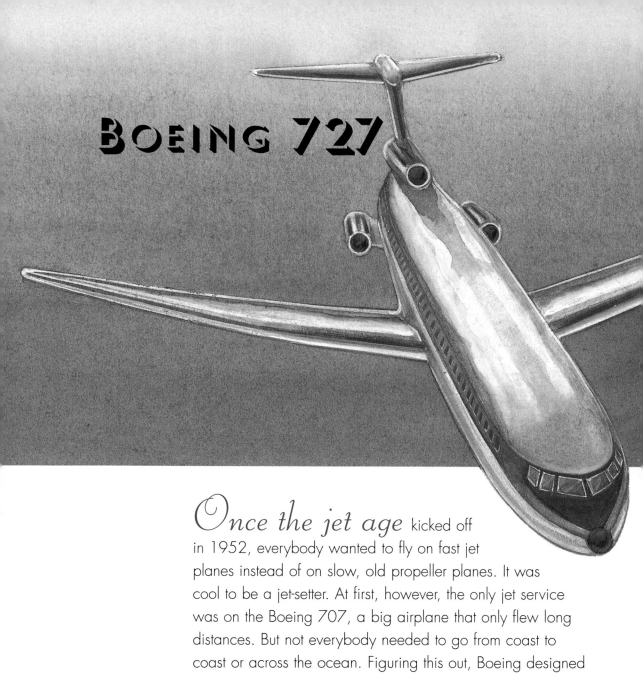

BOEING 727

Once the jet age kicked off
in 1952, everybody wanted to fly on fast jet
planes instead of on slow, old propeller planes. It was
cool to be a jet-setter. At first, however, the only jet service
was on the Boeing 707, a big airplane that only flew long
distances. But not everybody needed to go from coast to
coast or across the ocean. Figuring this out, Boeing designed
a smaller jet plane called the 727.

The 727 TRIJET, or three-engine jet, was a big hit. In no
time, airlines all over the world were flying 727s. For over

35 years, more 727s were in the air than any other airplane, and even though they're old now, most 727s are still flying.

The 727 is easy to spot. It has a unique T-shaped tail that helps it climb, fly, and descend quickly, making the airplane perfect for people who want to go shorter distances and get there fast. One of the engines sits right smack in front of the tail and the other two are attached to the sides of the airplane just below it, instead of hanging under the wings as on most jetliners. With the engines way in back, all the engine noise is in the back, too, making the 727 so quiet inside that Eastern Airlines advertised it as their "Whisper Jet."

The 727 can fly about 600 miles per hour, a huge improvement over Charles Lindbergh's plodding pace across the Atlantic of about 108 miles per hour.

For more than 20 years, Boeing built about as many versions of 727s as there are flavors of ice cream. There are 727 passenger planes, 727 cargo planes, and even one model that carries passengers during the day and quickly converts to carry cargo at night. They even stretched the 727 to make it 20 feet longer.

The 727 was so important in airplane history that the first one ever built is now in an airplane museum.

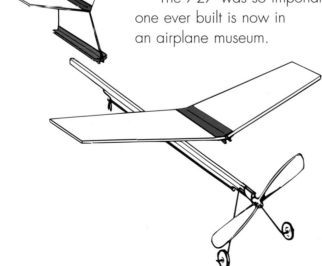

Snap on the wings with the dark green clip and the tail with the pink and brown clips.

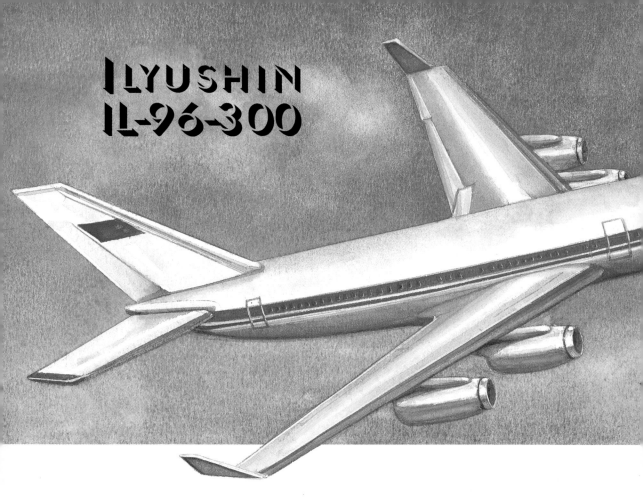

ILYUSHIN IL-96-300

$\mathcal{W}hen$ *wide-body airplanes* such as the Boeing 747 were developed, almost everybody wanted to fly in them because they were comfortable, fast, and you could take long hikes up and down the aisles. The Russians designed their own wide-body airplane called the ILYUSHIN IL-96-300 (say ILL-EE-YOU-SHUN).

The IL-96-300 is named after Sergei Ilyushin, the "father" of Russian aviation. He started out as a mechanic, but he went back to school to study engineering. Sergei found that designing gliders was easy, so he moved on to making World War II

16 AMAZING AIRPLANES

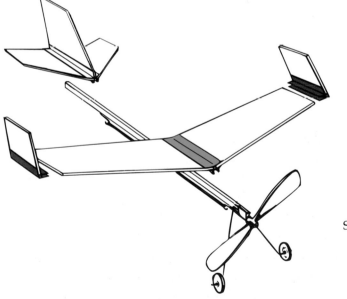

fighters and bombers, and then came up with ideas for Russia's first passenger planes.

The modern-day IL-96-300 is a very high-tech machine about the same size as the Boeing 777 or the Airbus A-330. Like them, it has "FLY BY WIRE" controls that send the pilot's commands electrically, using computers, instead of mechanically, using steel cables. But what makes the Ilyushin really cool are its WINGLETS, or flipperlike wingtips. Regular airplane wings create little whirlpools of air that swirl around the wingtips as the plane moves through the air, but the IL-96-300's winglets cut into the whirlpools and flatten them out. This gives the airplane more LIFT so the engines don't have to work as hard and the airplane doesn't burn as much fuel. Less fuel means less cost, so winglets have become popular on some private jets too.

The latest model of the Ilyushin IL-96-300 is an example of the new friendship between the United States and Russia. The engines and AVIONICS, or electronics systems, are made in America, while the rest of the plane is made in Russia.

Snap on the wings with the dark green clip and the tail with the white clip. Attach the winglets with the gray clips to the ends of the wings.

F-16

QUICK EXIT

F-16 pilots strap on a backpack loaded with a parachute and a survival kit before they get into the plane. If things go bad during air combat, they may have to exit the airplane really fast— through the roof—using the rocket-powered EJECTION SEAT.

When military leaders saw how effective air combat could be in wartime, they began using more and more airplanes instead of sending huge armies of soldiers out to fight each other on the ground. FIGHTERS and BOMBERS were the most important airplanes in the new AIR FORCE. Fighters are designed to be fast and agile, making quick strikes against targets on land or chasing and shooting at enemy airplanes in one-on-one air battles called DOGFIGHTS.

The most famous modern dogfight aircraft is the F-16, called the "Fighting Falcon." It's a supersonic hot rod—small, powerful, and very fast—twice the speed of sound. Swept-back wings make the F-16 stable and very nimble.

There's only one seat in the F-16, so the pilot has to fly the plane, fire missiles, shoot the gun, and dodge the enemy all at the same time. Fortunately for the pilot, the F-16's RUDDERS, AILERONS, and ELEVATORS are all controlled by computers. In fact, a human would react so much slower than a computer that if the pilot turned the computer off in flight, the plane would probably crash within seconds.

When you're zooming up and down in a roller coaster, you can feel your body—especially your stomach—seem to sink right down into your shoes. That's called PULLING G's, and the force of that pull is measured as G-FORCE.

F-16 pilots feel G-force in a big way. They're making so many quick, steep turns that the G-force actually pulls on their blood, forcing it down from their heads and into their stomachs and legs. If your brain doesn't get a steady flow of blood, you faint, something you don't want to do when you're moving at twice the speed of sound. That's why F-16 pilots wear flight suits called G-SUITS that fit tightly around their stomachs and legs. The suits have air pockets that automatically inflate when the plane makes a steep turn, squeez-ing the pilot's body and forcing blood back up to the brain.

Snap on the wings with the yellow clip and the tail with the white clip, and tape on a flight deck.

CONCORDE

In 1947, pilot Chuck Yeager experienced life in the fast lane—he flew a rocket airplane at SUPERSONIC speed, or faster than the speed of sound.

It took another 20 years for a team of British and French to build a passenger jet that could go that fast, but when they finally did, the Concorde could fly twice the speed of sound, or Mach 2 (say MOCK).

There's a good reason why the Concorde looks like Big Bird. Its beaklike nose is hinged so it can swing down and let the pilot see out the front when the plane is sitting on the ground, taking off, or landing, then swing up when airborne

THE CHOSEN FEW

The Concorde isn't very big compared to most other jetliners. It carries about 128 people, just a fourth of the passengers who fit into a 747 jumbo jet. Most of the people who fly in the Concorde are rich or famous—and sometimes both—or in a really big hurry, because tickets are very expensive.

to reduce drag. The swept-back triangular wing, called a DELTA wing, increases lift so the Concorde can climb quickly to cruise at 60,000 feet—almost twice as high as other passenger planes.

Getting from New York to London in about three hours has its advantages, but the Concorde has problems too. To begin with, a new Concorde has a humongous price tag. But even if an airline can afford to buy one, feeding it is another story. The Concorde might have been better named the "Vulture" because it sucks up three times more fuel—while carrying lots fewer people—than a 747. This does not earn it big points for energy conservation. To make matters worse, some scientists worry that burning all that fuel in the upper stratosphere damages the ozone layer that protects us from the sun's ultraviolet rays. The Concorde is also the loudest passenger plane ever made. As it approaches and breaks the speed of sound, the airplane gets pounded around by shock waves in the air that cause a SONIC BOOM with enough force to break windows and stress out cows so much that they stop producing milk. That's why Concordes are not allowed to fly over the United States.

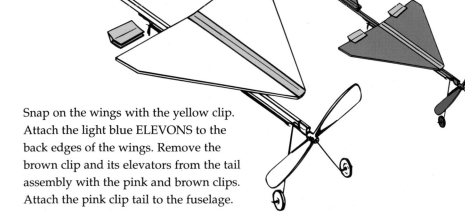

Snap on the wings with the yellow clip. Attach the light blue ELEVONS to the back edges of the wings. Remove the brown clip and its elevators from the tail assembly with the pink and brown clips. Attach the pink clip tail to the fuselage.

GLIDER

In the early 1800s, Sir George Cayley, a British inventor, built the first successful glider. He was smart enough not to fly in it himself since it crashed frequently, and he was also smart enough to think up the science of AERODYNAMICS, the study of how air moves around objects like birds, sails, and dogs with their heads hanging out car windows.

A few years later, would-be flyers were building airplanes that looked like giant kites with wings made of strong cloth stretched over wire and wood frames. The planes looked great, but couldn't move an inch on a day with no wind.

Almost a hundred years passed before people

successfully flew in gliders, but success to these early pilots meant a flight about the length of a football field with absolutely no way to control direction or altitude. This was a problem, and few glider pilots lived to a ripe old age. Gliders clearly were not a practical means of transportation.

Two bicycle manufacturers, Orville and Wilbur Wright, began their aviation careers building gliders and flying them at Kitty Hawk, North Carolina, where the wind blows hard and the sandy beaches cushioned their crash landings. When their bruises healed, they figured out a way to control the plane's movements, added an engine, and flew their way into history books.

Early gliders were launched by rolling them downhill to gain speed or by towing them with a rope. Today, gliders are towed into the air by airplanes with engines, then set free to fly gracefully like a bird, which was the whole idea in the first place. People fly gliders for fun and excitement— if there are lots of air currents and the pilot knows how to work the elevators, ailerons, and rudder, a glider can stay in the air for hours. It is doubtful, however, that your model glider will stay in the air for hours, because there is no skilled glider pilot inside.

Remove the rubber band, propeller, and landing gear from the fuselage. Snap on the wings with the red clip and the tail with the orange clip. Mold some clay (about the size of a marble) around the nose of the fuselage to balance the airplane in flight. Experiment with flying the glider. You may have to add or remove clay to make it fly well.

AMAZING AIRPLANES

FLIGHT TEST

You may want to start with the *Spirit of St. Louis*, the *Constellation*, or the *F-16*—they're the easiest to fly.

Flight tests are mostly by trial and error. Watch your airplane carefully on its first flights and make adjustments when you see problems, such as a headlong crash right after takeoff. Slowly but surely you'll find that by adjusting wing position, you can get your airplanes to stay in the air a long time!

Here are some flying tips from real pilots:

•**BALANCE** is really important! Look down at the plane from above: Each half of the plane should look exactly alike.

•Wings usually work best when attached about a third of the way back on the fuselage. *The Constellation is an exception—move its wings farther back.* A good way to test for wing balance is to hold the wing tips lightly between your fingertips—the fuselage should be level.

Hold like this for the delta wings.

Hold like this for all the other wings.

AMAZING AIRPLANES

- If the plane flies upward, dips, and then climbs again, the wings are too far forward. If the plane takes a nosedive and crashes, they're too far back.
- The calmer the day, the better your chances for a smooth flight. If there's a breeze, toss some leaves into the air to see where it's coming from, then launch your plane straight into the wind.
- The best place to fly is in a field or park where crash landings are a little softer and there's less traffic.

Avoid streets and watch for cars!
- Avoid flying near trees and stay away from power lines!

GETTING READY TO TAKE OFF:

- Wind up the propeller by spinning it clockwise with your finger and causing "knots" to form on the rubber band. Three layers of knots work great. The first layer of knots should just be a simple twist. On the second layer, the twists will twist on top of themselves to make lumpy knots, and on the third, the knots will twist on top of themselves again.

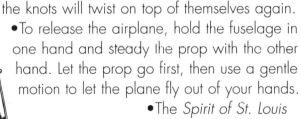

- To release the airplane, hold the fuselage in one hand and steady the prop with the other hand. Let the prop go first, then use a gentle motion to let the plane fly out of your hands.
- The *Spirit of St. Louis* and 727 can do ground takeoffs. Just be sure they're on a smoother surface. You'll also need to move the wings forward a little to help the plane climb faster.

Aerodynamics
HOW A PLANE FLIES

An airplane sitting on a runway is held down by GRAVITY, the invisible force that pulls everything toward the center of the Earth, including your toast when it falls jelly-side down onto the kitchen floor. Birds flap their wings and push air down to give them upward movement, or LIFT, but airplane wings don't flap. Airplanes get lift from the air that flows past their wings as they move forward.

How? The top of an airplane wing is curved in a shape called an AIRFOIL. When the airplane moves forward, the wing cuts the air in two pieces. The top air has to race across the curved surface while the bottom air moves straight ahead. Air has weight, or PRESSURE, that pushes down on us all the time. The faster-moving air on top of the wing presses down with less force, or lower PRESSURE, than the air underneath. High pressure always moves toward low pressure (that's a law of nature), so the air underneath the wing moves toward the lower pressure on top of the wing, pushing the airplane upward. The curved top and flat bottom of a Frisbee work

LIFT

DRAG

THRUST

GRAVITY

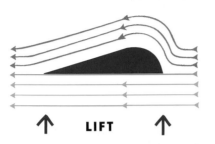

Faster-moving air, which creates less pressure.

LIFT

Slower-moving air, which creates more pressure.

the same way, unless the Frisbee is in your dog's mouth.

Moving wings can lift an airplane into the air, but if the plane doesn't keep moving, it will drop like a rock. Most airplanes have propellers or jet engines to produce THRUST. Thrust overcomes the air resistance called DRAG that opposes the airplane's forward movement. Drag also is what pulls your baseball cap off when you're riding your bike super fast.

Propeller blades are shaped like skinny little wings and work like a fan. As the propeller spins, the air pressure in front of the blades drops and the high-pressure air behind the blades pushes them—and the plane—forward.

Jet engines use a huge fan to suck air in, then scrunch it down until it's under a lot of pressure, burn fuel to heat it up, and blow it out the back, pushing the airplane forward. The effect is a lot like letting go of a blown-up balloon. Actually, squids came up with a backward idea of jet propulsion millions of years ago. They suck water into their bodies, then force it out through forward-pointing nozzles to propel themselves backward.

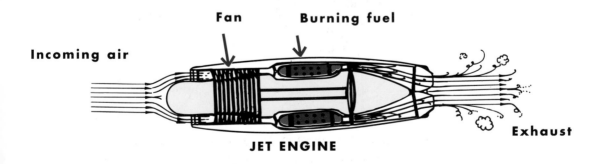

Fan   **Burning fuel**

Incoming air

Exhaust

JET ENGINE

Flying a Real Plane

ROLL

PITCH

YAW

Now that you understand all about gravity, lift, thrust, and drag—called AERODYNAMICS—you're ready to climb inside the cockpit, the low-tech name for FLIGHT DECK. From here you control parts of the wings and tail to make the airplane PITCH, ROLL, and YAW. Those are code words pilots use for the directions they steer the plane.

Here's how. The steering wheel in a plane isn't a wheel at all; it's a stick. It controls the plane as a steering wheel controls a car. Move the stick, or YOKE, forward and backward to move the ELEVATORS on the tail up and down. This makes the airplane's nose and tail go up and down, or PITCH, just like a teeter-totter.

PITCH

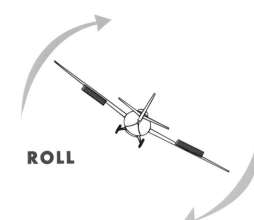

ROLL

If you move the yoke from side to side, the AILERONS on the wings move up and down and the airplane will ROLL as one wingtip dips lower, and the other wing goes up. Do this for very long and you'll probably need one of those little white airsick bags.

Now push on the RUDDER PEDALS. As you move the tail RUDDER back and forth, the nose of the plane turns, or YAWS, right or left, sort of like how a car turns a corner.

YAW

Sound easy? There's a catch: You have to work all the controls at the same time. There you are in the captain's seat, right hand on the THROTTLE, controlling speed and thrust, left hand on the yoke, controlling pitch and roll, and feet on the rudder pedals, controlling yaw. If this seems complicated, think how Orville Wright must have felt. He didn't have a yoke or rudder pedals—or even a captain's seat or a cap with an emblem on it. Instead, he connected cables from the wings to his belt, lay down on the lower wing of his airplane, twisted his hips to control the airplane's movement, and hung on for dear life. But it worked, and the basic flight control system he and brother Wilbur invented is still used today.

HIGHLIGHTS IN AIRPLANE HISTORY

People have wanted to fly ever since they looked up and saw birds. Early inventors who were obsessed with flight were easy to spot with their bruises and broken bones from crash landings.

Greek mythology has it that Icarus (ICK-A-RUS) and his father, Daedalus (DAY-DA-LUS), tried to fly by sticking feathers to their arms using wax. This worked swell until Icarus flew too close to the sun, which melted the wax, dropping him into the sea to become aviation's first splashdown. Even though it was a make-believe story, it got people to think about flight.

While Columbus was off discovering America in 1492, an Italian named Leonardo da Vinci came up with an idea of a flying machine with flapping wings called an ORNITHOPTER. This was truly a radical idea in his day—a machine that could fly! It's a good thing

Leonardo da Vinci's ornithopter

da Vinci made it big as an artist because the ornithopter never got off the ground.

The hottest idea in the early 1800s was the hot air balloon. Hot air is less dense, or lighter, than normal air, so heating the air inside a balloon causes it to float. But heating the air with an open-flame burner too close to the balloon fabric causes it to catch on fire, making early hot air ballooning a risky sport.

Wright brothers' biplane

In 1903, two bicycle manufacturers, Orville and Wilbur Wright, had the right idea. They designed a BIPLANE, with two wings, and curved them like birds' wings to create the upward force called lift. Being optimists, they named the airplane "Flyer." It had an engine about the same size as a lawn mower's. Even though the Flyer flew for only 12 seconds on its first flight, Orville was in control the whole time, and that was a real first in aviation. Within a few years, Orville and Wilbur's flights lasted more than a half hour and went up to 20 miles before they ran out of gas. The flying part was easy—it was landing that was dangerous until they figured out that wheels worked better as landing gear than wood runners shaped like skis.

Blériot's VII monoplane

A Frenchman named Louis Blériot (BLAIR-EE-OH) made history when he flew the first international flight in 1909—from France to England, all of 23 miles. He went on to design the first MONOPLANE, or single-wing aircraft, with an enclosed body and tail, and landing gear wheels. It looked good and

Dogfight

served as the basis for aircraft to come, but it didn't fly worth beans.

When World War I started in 1914, airplanes were still a new idea, but after four years of war, military aircraft had become fast and efficient. At first, airplanes were used for locating enemy forces, but once pilots figured out how to shoot at the enemy without shooting off their own propellers, they tried to knock each other out of the air in chases called DOGFIGHTS.

The Red Baron got his name by painting his airplane red, which seems logical. He flew the deadliest plane of the war, the German Fokker (FAWK-ER), against the Allied Forces' Sopwith Camel, a truly weird name unless you know that Sir Thomas Sopwith designed it with a hump over the gun cover. Meanwhile, in Russia, a flyer named Igor Sikorsky (SEE-KOR-SKI) designed the first really big airplane that could actually fly, a four-engine machine that went 60 miles per hour. In those days, that was fast.

Sopwith Camel

Traveling by airplane became the cool thing to do in the 1920s and 1930s. World War I pilots bought leftover warplanes and toured the country, showing off the flying skills they had learned during the war. Called BARNSTORMERS, they dazzled crowds with exciting feats of skill and daring,

Sikorsky's four-engine plane le Grand

such as flying through barn doors, walking on wings, and leaping from plane to plane. Lots of pilots who survived the war didn't survive barnstorming.

Now that airplanes didn't have to carry bombs, there was room for people. Soon airplanes had bathrooms, flight attendants, and meals on board. Back then, weight and balance were so critical for a safe flight that passengers, as well as their luggage, were weighed in before boarding.

Barnstorming

In 1927, Charles A. Lindbergh won $25,000 for being the first to fly alone across the Atlantic Ocean. Exactly five years later, Amelia Earhart became the first woman to do the same thing. She set a record for speed, crossing the ocean in less than half the time it took Lindbergh. Having a newer, faster airplane helped. In 1933, an American named Wiley Post took off alone and kept on going all the way around the world. He stopped many times to rest and refuel, and returned eight days later.

The first widely used passenger plane was the Douglas DC-3 built in 1936. It carried 21 passengers and went about 170 miles an hour. Some DC-3s are still being flown in parts of the world.

Amelia Earhart

AMAZING AIRPLANES

When World War II came along, new military aircraft were designed that flew faster, higher, and were deadlier than ever before. Some of the airplanes that were famous in the war and in old movies include the American B-17 Flying Fortress and B-29 bomber, the British Spitfire, the German Messerschmitt Bf 109 and the Japanese Mitsubishi A6M Zero.

B-29 bomber

After World War II, the United States and Russia wanted fast, high-tech bombers, fighters, and spy planes so they could threaten each other and keep the Cold War exciting, so engineers got busy designing JET ENGINES.

Jet engines worked so well on military planes that friendly airlines wanted them for passenger flights too. The British Comet was the first passenger jet, but it had an unfortunate habit of exploding in flight, so it never became very popular.

New technology in the 1930s led to more improvements—radios were better, RADAR was developed and cabins were PRESSURIZED to allow airplanes to fly at high altitudes where the air was thin and difficult to breathe. Automatic controls, or AUTOPILOTS, let pilots fly in bad weather even when they couldn't see a foot in front of their faces.

Yeager's Bell B-1

In 1947, Air Force Captain Chuck Yeager flew a rocket airplane faster than the speed of sound, paving the way for supersonic flight. But it wasn't until 1968 that the Russians flew a TU-144, the first

34

AMAZING AIRPLANES

SUPERSONIC TRANSPORT that could carry lots of people. Today, the only SST in operation is the Concorde.

The jet age was launched in 1958 with Boeing 707 service between the United States and Europe. Lots of different models of jet passenger planes were built in the 1960s, and in 1970, the 747 jumbo jet was introduced. It can carry nearly 500 passengers.

Space shuttles are airplanes powered by rockets. Once launched, it takes about 15 minutes for them to reach orbital altitude, then they zoom round and round the Earth at about 16,600 miles per hour before returning to Earth to land like a glider.

Boeing 747

Future airplane travel will probably include flying from space station to space station, to other planets, or just cruising around the solar system. Creative thinkers already have plans for solar-powered airplanes that run on electricity from the sun and laser planes powered by laser beams from space. Back on Earth, individual airplanes will probably be as common as the family car and as easy to operate as your bicycle or computer.

Space shuttle Challenger

The main hang-up on all these great ideas is fuel. There's not much oil left on Earth and what's here is very expensive, so before you can start flying to school, we need to find a cheaper, environmentally friendly way to propel airplanes.

Future aircraft Lockheed Mach-4

AMAZING AIRPLANES

ORDERING EXTRA PARTS

If you accidentally sent your F-16 careening into the ground at full speed or the dog mistook your Concorde for a Frisbee and caught it in midflight, your airplanes probably got a little scuffed up—or worse. After all, experimental flight can be dangerous!

When airplane manufacturers such as Boeing or Airbus build airplanes, they always make extra parts, called SPARES, so airplanes can be quickly and easily fixed when something breaks or is damaged. You can get spares for your airplanes too.

SIG Manufacturing offers a replacement parts package that includes all the airplane parts that came in *The Amazing Airplanes Book & Kit*.

Replacement parts cost $9.95, including shipping.

SIG Manufacturing accepts checks, money orders, MasterCard, or Visa as payment.

You can phone, fax, or mail your order to:
SIG Manufacturing Co., Inc.
401-7 S. Front Street
Montezuma, IA 50171
Phone 1-800-247-5008
Fax   1-515-623-3922